HAL•LEONARD

Pro Vocal®

BETTER THAN KARAOKE!

VOLUME 63

JERSEY BOYS

SING 8 SONGS WITH SOUND-ALIKE AUDIO TRACKS

To access audio visit:
www.halleonard.com/mylibrary

Enter Code
1241-3756-2666-6621

ISBN 978-1-4950-0079-9

HAL•LEONARD®
CORPORATION
7777 W. BLUEMOUND RD. P.O. BOX 13819 MILWAUKEE, WI 53213

JERSEY BOYS

Big Girls Don't Cry

Words and Music by Bob Crewe and Bob Gaudio

Am7 D7 G E7 Am7 D7
(My, oh my.) My girl did - n't
G C G N.C. E7
cry.) (I won - der why.) (Sil - ly boy.) Told my girl we
A7
had to break up. (Sil - ly boy.) Thought that she would call my bluff. (Sil - ly
D7 G Bm/D
boy.) Then she said, to my sur - prise, "Big girls
C D7 G E7 Am7 D7
don't cry." Big girls don't
G E7 Am7 D7 G E7
cry - y - y. (They don't cry.) Big girls

Am7 D7 G E7 Am7 D7
don't cry. (That's just an al - i - bi.)
G Em Am D7 G Em
Am D7 G E7 Am7 D7
May - be I was
G E7 Am7 D7 G E7
cruel. (I was cruel.) Ba - by,
Am7 D7 G C G N.C.
I'm a fool.) (I'm such a fool.) Sil - ly
E7 A7
girl.) Shame on you, your ma - ma said. (Sil - ly girl.) Shame on you, you're

D7
cry'n' in bed. (Sil - ly girl.) Shame on you, you told a lie.
G Bm/D C D7 G E7
Big girls do cry. Big girls
Am7 D7 G E7 Am7 D7
don't cry - y - y. (They don't cry.)
G E7 Am7 D7 G E7
Big girls don't cry. (That's just an
Am7 D7 G Bm/D C D7 G Bm/D
al - i - bi.) Big girls don't cry, Big girls
C D7 G Bm/D C D7 G
don't cry, big girls don't cry.

Bye Bye Baby
(Baby Goodbye)

Words and Music by Bob Crewe and Bob Gaudio

D D6 Dmaj7 D6
now if I were free. I wish it could
A E A
be. I could love you, but why be - gin it,
D D+
'cause there ain't an - y fu - ture in it, see.
(She's got me and
D6 Ddim7 G♭
Bye, bye, ba - by, ba - by, good -
I'm not free, so...)
A♭m7 D♭ G♭
bye. Bye, bye,
A♭m7 D♭
ba - by, don't make me cry.
A
Guess I nev - er will know you bet - ter. Wish I knew you be -
D D6 Dmaj7 D6
fore I met her. Gee, how good you would

A E A
be for me. Should have told you that
I can't lin - ger. There's a wed - ding ring on my fin - ger,
D D+ D6 Ddim7 G♭
see. Bye, bye,
(She's got me and I'm not free, so...)
A♭m7 D♭
ba - by, ba - by, good - bye.
G♭ A♭m7
Bye, bye, ba - by, don't make me cry.
D♭ A Bm7
Oh, ah.
E7 A
Bye,
Repeat and Fade
Bm7 E7
ba - by, bye. Bye,

Can't Take My Eyes Off of You

Words and Music by Bob Crewe and Bob Gaudio

G7
Bbm6
F
good to be true, can't take my eyes off of you.
F/C
F
Par - don the way that I stare, _ there's noth - ing
Fmaj7
F9
else to com - pare. _ The sight of you leaves me weak,
Bb
there are no words left to speak. But if you
Bbm
F
feel like I feel, please let me know that it's real.
G7
Bbm6
You're just too good to be true, can't take my
F
Gm7b5 Gm7 Gm7b5 Gm7
eyes off of you.

B♭m/C Gm7/C F+ F6 F+ F6 F+ F6
Gm7♭5 Gm7 Gm7♭5 Gm7 B♭m/C Gm7/C F+ F6 F+ F6
D7♯9 D5 Gm7
I love you, ba - by, and if it's
C7 F Dm7
quite all right, I need you, ba - by, to warm the lone-ly night. I love you,
Gm7 Gm7/C C7 F6
ba - by, trust in me when I say:
Dm7 Gm7 C7
Oh, pret - ty ba - by, don't bring me down, I pray. Oh, pret - ty
F Dm7 Gm7
ba - by, now that I've found you, stay, and let me love you, ba -

E♭9 E♭7 C7
- by. Let me love you. You're just too
F Fmaj7
good to be true, can't take my eyes off of you.
F9
You'd be like heav - en to touch, I wan - na
B♭ B♭m
hold you so much. At long last love has ar - rived,
F
and I thank God I'm a - live. You're just too
G7 B♭m6 F
good to be true, can't take my eyes off of you.
Gm7♭5 Gm7 Gm7♭5 Gm7 B♭m/C Gm7/C

F+ F6 F+ F6 D7♯9 D5
I love you,
Gm7 C7 F
ba - by, and if it's quite all right, I need you, ba - by, to warm the
Dm7 Gm7 Gm7/C C7
lone - ly night. I love you, ba - by, trust in me when I
F6 Dm7 Gm7
say: Oh, pret - ty ba - by, don't bring me
C7 F Dm7
down, I pray. Oh, pret - ty ba - by, now that I've found you, stay, and let me
Gm7 E♭9 E♭7
love you, ba - by. Let me love you.
N.C. E♭9
You're just too good to be true...

December 1963
(Oh, What a Night)

Words and Music by Robert Gaudio and Judy Parker

B♭ E♭ F B♭ E♭
be the same. What a la - dy, what a night.
F Cm E♭ E♭maj7
Oh, I, I got a fun - ny feel - in' when she
Gm F Cm
walked in the room. Yeah, my, as
E♭ F6
3
I re - call it end - ed much too soon. (Oh, what a night!)
B♭ E♭ F7 B♭ E♭
Hyp - no - tiz - ing, mes - mer - iz - in' me,
F B♭ E♭ F
she was ev - 'ry - thing I dreamed she'd be. Sweet sur - ren - der, what a night.
B♭ E♭ B♭/F E♭/F Gm C
Gm C Gm C C7 Dm

Eb F7 Bb
(Oh, what a night!)
Eb F7 Bb Eb F
Why'd it take so long to see the light? It seemed so wrong, but now it
Bb Eb F
seems so right. Sweet sur - ren - der, what a night.
Bb Cm7 Dm7
I felt a rush like a roll - in' ball of thun - der,
Eb F
spin - nin' my head a - round and tak - in' my bod - y un - der.
Bb Eb F Bb Eb
Oh, what a night!
F Bb Eb F
Oh, what a night! Oh, what a night!
Bb Eb F Bb
Oh, what a night!

Let's Hang On

Words and Music by Bob Crewe, Denny Randell and Sandy Linzer

G Am/G G
D/F♯
You say you're gon - na go and call it quits, gon - na
Am D Am
chuck it all and break our love to bits. (Break- in' up.) I wish you'd
D Am D
nev - er said it. No, no, we'll both re - gret it.
G D/F♯ Am
That lit - tle chip of dia-mond on your hand ain't a for - tune, ba - by, but you
D Am D
know it stands (for your love,) a love to try and bind us,
(Such a love)
Am D G
we just can't leave be - hind us. Ba - by, (don't you go,)

Gdim7 Am D G
ba - by, (no, no, no,) ba - by, stay - yay. Let's hang on
C/G G C/G G C G
to what we've got. Don't let go, girl, we've got a
D Am D Bm7 Em Am
lot. Got a lot of love be - tween us. Hang on,
D G Am/G G Am/G
hang on, hang on to what we've got.
G Am G D/F♯ Am
D G D/F♯ Am D

G D/F♯ Am
There is - n't an - y - thing I would - n't do, I'd pay an - y price to get in
D Am D
good with you. (Patch it up.) Give me a sec - ond turn in.
Am D G
Don't cool off while I'm burn - in'. You've got me cry - ing, dy - ing
D/F♯ Am D Am
at your door. Don't shut me out, let me in once more. (O - pen up)
D Am
your arms, I need to hold you.
(O - pen up) your heart, oh
D G Gdim7
girl, I told you. Ba - by, (don't you go,) ba - by, (no, no, no,)

Am D G C/G G
ba - by, stay - yay. Let's hang on to what we've got.
C/G G C G D
Don't let go, girl, we've got a lot. Got a
Am D Bm7 Em Am D
lot of love be - tween us. Hang on, hang on, hang on
G Am/G G Am/G G Am G
to what we've got.
D/F♯ Am D
G D/F♯ Am D G

My Eyes Adored You

Words and Music by Bob Crewe and Kenny Nolan

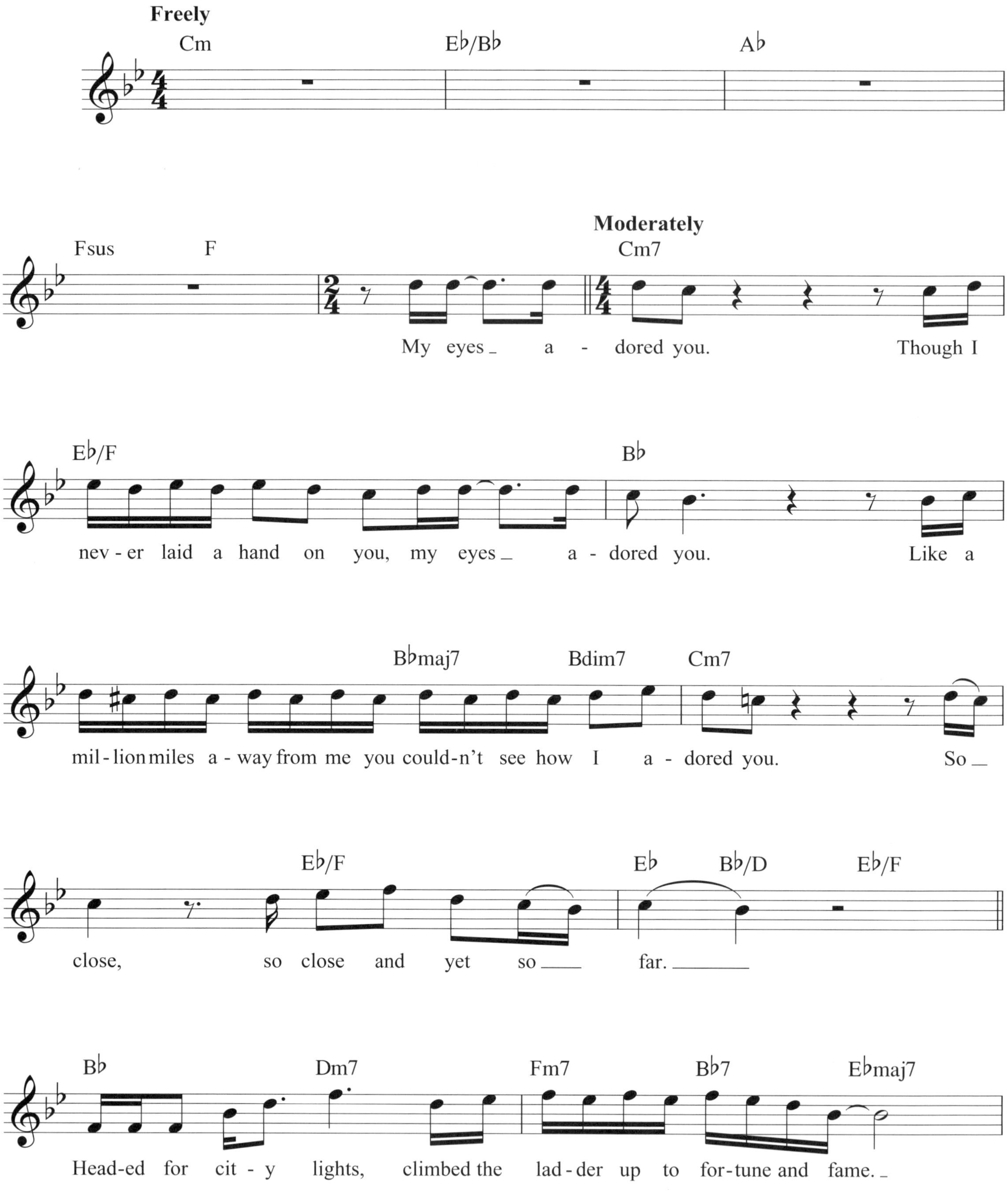

Cm7 A♭ F
Worked my fin - gers to the bone, made my - self a name.
Gm Dm7 Fm7 B♭7 E♭maj7
Fun-ny, I seem to find that no mat-ter how the years un - wind, still I
Cm7 A♭ C/G
rem - i - nisce 'bout the girl I miss and the love I left be -
Fsus F Cm7
hind. My eyes a - dored you. Though I
E♭/F B♭
nev - er laid a hand on you, my eyes a - dored you. Like a
B♭maj7 Bdim7 Cm7
mil - lion miles a - way from me you could-n't see how I a - dored you. So

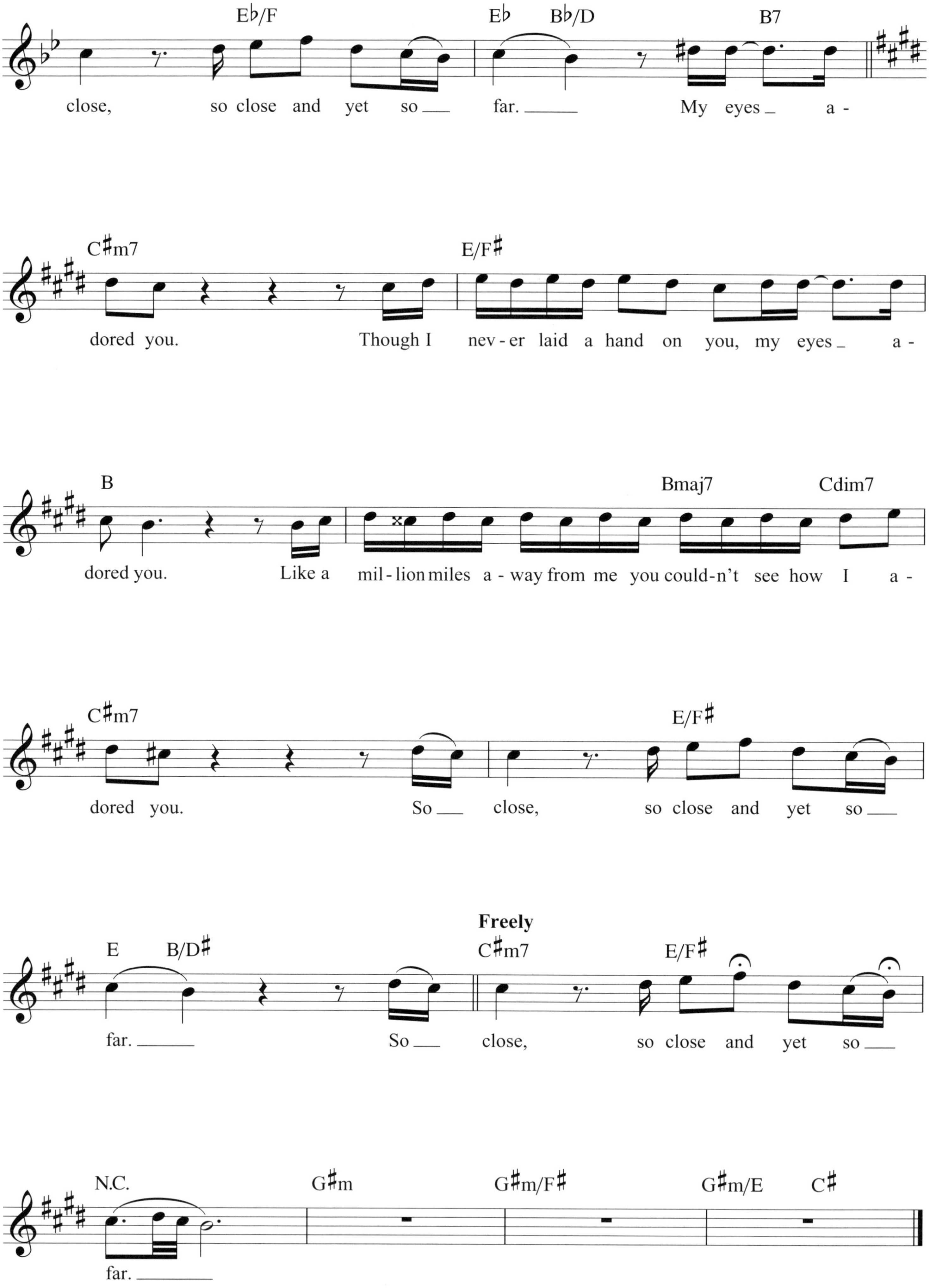
E♭/F
E♭ B♭/D
B7
close, so close and yet so far. My eyes a-
C♯m7
E/F♯
dored you. Though I nev-er laid a hand on you, my eyes a-
B
Bmaj7
Cdim7
dored you. Like a mil-lion miles a-way from me you could-n't see how I a-
C♯m7
E/F♯
dored you. So close, so close and yet so
E B/D♯
Freely
C♯m7
E/F♯
far. So close, so close and yet so
N.C.
G♯m
G♯m/F♯
G♯m/E C♯
far.

Sherry

Words and Music by Bob Gaudio

Dm7 G7 C Am Dm7 G7
(Sher - ry, ba - by.) Sher - ry, can you come out to -
C E♭ F C N.C. E7
night? (Why don't you come on,) to my
A7
Twist par - ty? (Come on,) where the bright moon shines.
D7 G7 N.C.
(Come on,) we'll dance the night a - way. I'm gon - na make you
G7 C Am Dm7 G7
mi - yi - yi - yine. Sher - ry,
C Am Dm7 G7 C Am
ba - by. (Sher - ry, ba - by.) Sher - ry,
Dm7 G7 C E♭ F C N.C.
can you come out to - night? (Why don't you

E7 A7
come on,) put your red dress on? (Come on,) mm, you
D7
look so fine. (Come on,) move it nice and eas - y.
G7 N.C. G7 C Am
Girl, you make me lose my mind. Sher -
Dm7 G7 C Am Dm7 G7
- ry, ba - by. (Sher - ry, ba - by.)
C Am Dm7 G7 C Am
Sher - ry, can you come out to - night? (Come, come,
Dm7 G7 C Am Dm7 G7
come out to - night.) Sher - ry, Sher - ry, ba - by.
C Am Dm7 G7 C Am
Sher - ry, Sher - ry, ba - by. Sher - ry,
Dm7 G7 C Am Dm7 G7 C
Sher - ry, ba - by.

Walk Like a Man

Words and Music by Bob Crewe and Bob Gaudio

B♭ Cm B♭ Cm B♭ Cm
tell - in' dirt - y lies to my friends. My own fa - ther said,
B♭ Cm B♭ Cm B♭ N.C.
"Give her up, don't both- er, the world is - n't com-ing to an end." (He said,)
E♭ E♭/G A♭ E♭ A♭ E♭ Gm
"Walk like a man, talk like a man, walk like a man, my
A♭ B♭ E♭ E♭/G A♭ E♭ A♭
son. No wom-an's worth crawl - in' on the earth, so
E♭ Gm A♭ F B♭ E♭
walk like a man, my son." Oo.
B♭ E♭ B♭ E♭ B♭ E♭
(Walk, walk, walk, walk.)
B♭ E♭ B♭ E♭ B♭ N.C.
Oo, ah. (Said,)

Eb Eb/G Ab Eb Ab Eb Gm
walk like a man, fast as I can, walk like a man from
Ab Bb Eb Eb/G Ab Eb Ab
3
you. I'll tell the world for - get a - bout it, girl,
Eb Gm Ab F Bb Eb
walk like a man from you. Oo.
Bb Eb Bb Eb Bb Eb
(Walk, walk, walk, walk.)
Bb Eb Bb Eb Bb
Oo. Walk
Eb/Bb Bb F Eb
like a man, like
F Bb
a man.